Insearch of Mickey Mantle

Insearch of Mickey Mantle

NEW AND SELECTED POEMS

. . .

Logan C. Jones

RESOURCE *Publications* • Eugene, Oregon

INSEARCH OF MICKEY MANTLE
New and Selected Poems

Copyright © 2024 Logan C. Jones, EdD. All rights reserved. Except for brief quotations in critical publications or reviews, no part of this book may be reproduced in any manner without prior written permission from the publisher. Write: Permissions, Wipf and Stock Publishers, 199 W. 8th Ave., Suite 3, Eugene, OR 97401.

Resource Publications
An Imprint of Wipf and Stock Publishers
199 W. 8th Ave., Suite 3
Eugene, OR 97401

www.wipfandstock.com

PAPERBACK ISBN: 978-1-4982-3599-0
HARDCOVER ISBN: 978-1-4982-3601-0
EBOOK ISBN: 978-1-4982-3600-3

All rights reserved. No part of the book may be reproduced or used in any manner without the written permission of the copyright owner except for the use of quotations in a book review.

For Caleb

If we discover the place of the soul—
and the experience of God—
to be darkly within and below,
we must reckon with a perilous voyage.
— James Hillman

All of the heavens and all of the hells are within you.
— Joseph Campbell

Contents

Lord of the Sea 1
The Music of Heaven 2
Translating Rilke 3
Blue Ridge Fog 4
Lord, Remind Me 6
The Edge of the Underworld 7
Wide Awake 9
Holiday Inn 11
My Friend Died Today 14
Moonrise at Nags Head 15
No Man's Land 16
All God's Children Gotta Cry 18
Four Deer 20
Living Without You 21
Calling 24
Lonesome Seagull 25
Fire and Laughter 26
The Alchemy of Healing 28
Other Words 30
Abandoned 31
Marked 32
The Antidote to Pain 33

Inner Neighbors 34
No Reason to Hold Back 37
Change of Heart 38
Both Are True 39
The Tree of Life 40
The Unraveling 41
Angels Everywhere 42
And He Shall Reign Forever and Ever 43
Gizmo 44
Prepare to Meet Thy God 45
Once There Was a Time 46
Insearch of Mickey Mantle 48
Wind, Stars . . . Moon 51
Cardiac Rehab 52
Shell-shocked 53
Climate Change 54
Overlook 55
Under a Full Moon on Christmas Eve 56
On the Way Home 57
November Afternoon 58
Waiting on the Moon 59
Young Children Know 60
O Christmas Tree 61
Boys, Get Your Coats 62
Christmas Morning on Church Street 63
Do Not Be Afraid 65
Lord, I Believe . . . 66
One More Day 67
Christmas Lights 68
Heaven Was a Friend to Her 69
DNA Wins 70

My Heart Is Not Failing 71
Create in Me, O God 73
No Job Title 74
What Are You Going to Do Now? 75
Misty Trail 76
Rumi and Rilke 77
Five Hawks and a Jet 78
Rainbow 79
Easter Moon 80
Callie Mae 81
Take the Pain 82
If I Were a Wise Man 84
Leviathan 87
Three Voices 88
Son of David, Son of Joseph 90
The Journey Home 92

Acknowledgements

I WISH TO THANK the editors of the following publications in which the following poems previously appeared.

"Translating Rilke": Reprinted with permission from *The Best of James Hollis: Wisdom for the Inner Journey,* Chiron Publications, Asheville, NC.

"No Man's Land," "The Antidote to Pain," "Under a Full Moon on Christmas Eve," "Three Voices," "Easter Moon," and "The Music of Heaven": Reprinted with permission from *No Man's Land: Poems,* Resource Publications, Eugene, OR.

"And He Shall Reign Forever and Ever," "The Alchemy of Healing," "Lord, I Believe...," and "Son of David, Son of Joseph": Reprinted with permission from *Last Call: Poems,* Resource Publications, Eugene, OR.

Scripture quotations are from Revised Standard Version of the Bible, copyright Ó 1946, 1952, and 1971, National Council of the Churches of Christ in the United States of America. Used by permission. All rights reserved worldwide.

Lord of the Sea

He stands in the surf,
waves easily lapping at his knees.
Being sixteen months old, he looks further out to sea,
into the future where
the larger waves crash and roar.

He claps his hands, laughing.
He bends down and
splashes in the water,
then jumps up and down, dancing —
summoning the wind and the waves
to him.

His great delight is held with Joy and Gratitude.
Just for a moment, in the golden afternoon
at the end of summer,
all of the ocean belongs to him.
Just for a moment, he is Poseidon,

                              Lord of the Sea.

The Music of Heaven

Bach plays in heaven,
and Mannheim Steamroller
during the winter solstice,
and, of course, the Beatles.

But when the angels need
to smile,
they listen for Kelli's
laughter.

Her laughter comes from
a wellspring of gladness,
from a deep place
of delight,
of joy,
of ease,
of wonder.

Born out of loss
and the knowing of
God's acceptance,
Kelli's laughter
is the music
of heaven.

Translating Rilke

Rilke said:
You must change your life.

This is what he meant:
You must become
who you are meant to be —

or else die
a thousand deaths
each day.

Blue Ridge Fog

A dense, soupy fog settles
over the Blue Ridge,
hiding trees, roads, fields,
      even the way home.

You cannot see the road.
The way ahead is unclear.
You must slow down and
      pay attention.

Like Jonah, you are swallowed up.
The way home is hidden.
Yes, you do know something
      about hiding.

You have your many, many ways
to keep from being seen
and known by others —
      and yourself.

Of course, the fog burns off and lifts.
Now what?
Now you can see
      and you can be seen —

If you can be seen,
      then you can be known.

If you can be known,
      then you can be loved,

And if you can be loved,
> you can be forgiven.

Lord, Remind Me

Lord, remind me of my brokenness,
so I might honor the brokenness of others.

Remind me of my laugher,
so I might laugh with others.

Remind me of my dream,
so I might share the dream of others.

Remind me of my hauntedness,
so I might remember what it means to be called.

Remind me of my gifts,
so I might remember that the Kingdom is within.

Remind me of the uneasiness of faith,
so my doubts keep me searching.

Remind me of my journey, O Lord,
so I might remember the Wilderness, the Exile,

and the Homecoming.

Especially the Homecoming.

The Edge of the Underworld

You did not die.

But you did . . .
as you lay on the hard table
waiting for the catheter to
make its way to your heart.

You journeyed to the edge of
the Underworld.
But you did not know it then.
You only heard the music and

felt the tears spill from your eyes.
You were led to the waters of the
River of Memory
as the stents were placed

in your blocked vessels.
Later, you remembered
the call from far away
and from within:

Be who you are . . . no one else.
Trust the fire.
Hold on to this second chance.
Live your life differently.

      Do not be afraid of joy.

The River of Memory will

heal and restore you.
You will be reborn
at the edge of the Underworld.

Wide Awake

You lay on your right side,
then you flip over
and lay on your left.
You look at the clock.

Time moves slowly
into the deeper hours of the night.
You flip again
and lay on your back,

staring at the ceiling.
You are wide awake.
Why did you drink that iced tea at dinner?
What were you thinking?

You turn the pillow over to the cool side.
You pull the covers up,
then push them down.
Nothing works.

You flip some more.
Finally, you get up
to go the bathroom and
make your way back to the bed.

Sleep, like God, is elusive.
The night gets darker and
you wonder when blessed sleep will come,
even perchance to dream . . .

a healing dream
to help you

    find your way.

Holiday Inn

Why do they keep banging on the door at all hours?
Can't they read the friggin' sign?
It says No Vacancy
in flashing neon.
What's so hard about that?

Usually I send them on their way,
telling them to check with the Best Western
or the Hampton Inn.
Maybe the Marriot will have a room.
Just go away and let me go back to sleep.

But for some reason on this night,
this young couple got my attention.
They were in a rusted-out, broken-down, old El Camino.
I don't how it was still running.
When I opened the door, this young kid looked

like he was 17, maybe 18.
He was exhausted and about to cry.
The young girl, he said,
was pregnant.
They needed help, a place to stay for the night.

Something stirred in me.
I told this young man, this kid,
they could stay out back in the garage.
But there was no heat and no bedding.
I found some old blankets

and some leftovers in the refrig.
It was all I had.
My wife would have done more, I know.
She died a couple of years ago.
I still miss her.

The young man tried to give me $20
but I told him to keep it;
it looked like he needed it more than I did.
Thinking back, it was a strange night.
It was uncommonly bright.

It felt like all the stars were looking at me.
I opened the garage for them,
turned on the lights,
and let them be.
The young girl thanked me.

I tried to go back to sleep.
Maybe I did;
I am not sure.
I think I heard the sharp cry of a woman in labor,
the wail of a newborn infant,

> and the joy and relief of a new father.
> Then only a hush and thick silence.

It was cold.
I pulled the blankets up and rolled over.
Maybe no one else would show up tonight.
I thought I heard angels singing,
or was it all a dream?

It was all so strange.
Maybe one day someone
will help me understand
what it means...

My Friend Died Today

In Memoriam

Mary Oliver died today.
I sit here at my desk,
tears in my heart
re-feeling all of her words that
helped me,
loved me,
comforted me,
stunned me,
challenged me,

    and saved me.

She will always be my friend.

Moonrise at Nags Head

My old friend rises as
if coming out of the sea.
She has seen me through
many troubles over the years.
Even now, she still watches over me.
As I feel her rise,
she tells me and
my heart:

"You come from the stars.
The fire is within you.
It always has been.
Let the four stents in your heart
remind you to keep you soul open
to all of my secrets.
Let the meaning of your life be as thick
as your blood is now thin.

And when you are called home,

                you will return to the stars."

No Man's Land

The old farm house seemed huge,
mansion-like in all its secrets and
out-buildings with their weathered boards.
His room was upstairs
where it was hot and musty,
bathed in a yellow haze of light.
An old truck kept his gas mask,
cartridge belt, and helmet.

The helmet carried a dent
from a sniper's bullet
or so the story went in the family.

These war relics made for great battles
in the backyard where we would climb out
of the tranches, going over the top
into No Man's Land. Artillery shells would
burst overhead as tanks led the assault.
There would always be a mustard gas attack
which would leave us stricken and
flailing on the ground where we would
end up laughing. These battles
were epic and we never ran out
of tobacco sticks for rifles.
Our causalities always got up for lunch.

My grandfather was a sergeant
in a machine gun company
with the American Expeditionary Force
in France.

I never heard him speak of his war
and I never speak
of mine.

All God's Children Gotta Cry

The call came about one in the early morning.
Nothing good ever happens in those phone calls.
My sister was crying.
She said Dad had a heart attack.
They were at the Emergency Room.

She would call back.
I was half-way across the country.
I could not be there.
Maybe it was two hours later, maybe less,
but she called and just said, "He's gone."

Just like that, my dad had died and
I was not there to say goodbye.
The rest of those dark hours were a blur.
I do remember going back to bed,
hoping I would wake up from this nightmare.

As dawn broke, my wife was making
phone calls for airline tickets,
getting someone to take us to the airport.
She was taking care of our daughter.
My dad was dead — I had to get home.

Sometime that morning, our pastor came by the house.
I never knew how he knew.
He just came and sat with us around the breakfast table.
I don't remember him saying much;
he was simply and wonderfully there.

That was enough.
The flight home was a blur.
Some of my parents' good friends picked us up.
When we got the house,
I was stunned to see all the cars.

Cars filled the driveway,
parked on the grass,
parked on the side of the road.
I did not want to go in the house and
face all those people.

So I stood in the yard and
screamed silently
my anguish
for now being a fatherless son.
All God's children gotta cry.

All God's children gotta cry.

Four Deer

Coming out the door,
I heard them before I saw them.

They crashed through the trees,
announcing their presence.

Then shadowed against the darkened sky,
the four deer stopped and looked.

In the stillness of the complete number,
God showed up.

It seems God is always just out of reach,
but always near.

All we need to do is pay attention—
and look and listen,

        and even pray.

Living Without You

Are you still there, somewhere?
How I wish I could go home and
you would be in the kitchen,
busy, almost frantic,
bringing to life a meal of prodigal proportions.

Drinks are poured,
a fancy appetizer appears that we have never seen before
but now are required to try and enjoy.
The bounty set before us elegant,
overwhelming, brought to the table

with a love expressed sweetly,
in abundance overflowing
just as the laughter overflows.
I see my dad at the head of the table.
Jokes and stories surround the food,

All to sustain us,
to sustain me . . . yes,
to help me.
I never knew how to be
in my family.

I was too lost, not knowing
what I needed or wanted.
I left, searching, and did not know where to look.
I sought home, someplace where I belonged.
Maybe I always belonged.

But I did not understand it.
When my dad died, I was floundering.
I did not know how to connect with you.
My feelings confused me even more...
How did all this come to be?

How did it all come to pass?
A lost son without a father,
and now, I watch from a safe distance
as you, mother, live in your lost world.
I wish you were not frightened.

You always told me that everything would be OK.
Always. That was always your comment
And I hated it.
It always felt like you never heard
my deep pain and lostness...

And now as I watch, cringing in your presence,
pulling away at your touch,
not knowing even how to sit with you quietly,
I think: Everything will be OK.
It will. Soon, I hope...

Then I will have to learn to live without you.
I am afraid.
I do not know how to say goodbye.
I wish I could run into your arms
like I would do when I was five

And you would hold me,
rub my head,
pat me on the back —

and tell me everything is going to be OK.
I will live without you.

I will remember your love for me,
the ways you allowed me to leave.
I will always be grateful.

Calling

I don't have a real job anymore.
I retired — whatever that means —
and walked away.
It was time to get out of the way.

There was no need to hang on and
complain about all the changes
because changes have always been happening.
Nothing is new.

So I look at the blank page,
and try to feel what I feel.
I listen for the right word
and hope the gods will help me.

I don't have a real job anymore.
My work now is different.
It is time to trust my calling —
and the words.

Lonesome Seagull

Like memory, the ocean waves relentlessly deposit
debris and treasure on the shoreline
without measure.
Sometimes the waves slam violently,
just how memories sometimes slam on the soul.
Other times the waves, like memories, are gentle,
rolling in with quiet foam painting pictures on the sand.

A lonesome seagull stands watch
just at the edge of the surf.
Waves and memories never cease.
No one else is on this beach now.
Just a lonesome seagull
and a lonesome soul
with four stents in his heart,

each waiting,
each one living in gratitude.

Fire and Laughter

For John

When I first met John, I did not know enough
to be anxious or even scared.
We sat in his office,
feet propped up on the table,
and had an easy conversation
about my application to the pastoral care training program.

Only later did I learn
I should have been afraid.
John had a well-deserved reputation
for being hard and challenging.
He talked straight.
He neither took prisoners nor suffered fools.

But there was more: he always listened quietly to my grief over
all the children who died on the pediatric floor.
He never tried to fix my sorrow or solve it.
He simply and kindly honored it.
God, he pushed me — to be a better chaplain,
to be a better companion,

>   to be a better man.

John would not let me settle.
His fire, like his laughter, was healing.
When I finished the program, he blessed me —
deeply and authentically.
John believed in me and he believed I could do the work
I was being called to do.

John's blessing took hold of me and
changed my life

      forever.

The Alchemy of Healing

Strange work is underfoot
in the darkness,
filled with spells and incantations
and wild hope.
The primal elements are set loose
upon the earth,
upon my soul.

Ancient stories tell
of loosening up,
of unfreezing,
of being tested,
of standing firm,
of rising from ashes.

Through tears
and sorrow
and brokenness,
still searching
for a crumb of hope,
for understanding,
there persists
the longing for blessing
instead of curse.

There remains
the longing for embrace
that eases pain,
that gives golden courage
to try again

another day,
one more day.

One more time.

Other Words

The road sign says
Entering Virginia Entrepreneurial Zone

which is another way of saying Flea Market,
which means the same thing as Recycle Center,

which is another way of announcing a Second Chance,
which are other words for

Hope.

God knows we all need a Second Chance.
We all need Hope.

Abandoned

Abandoned farm homes sit
along the back roads
off the Blue Ridge Parkway.
They are collapsing in on themselves.

Windows are broken,
porches rotting,
roofs caving in by the unseen weight of emptiness,
wild weeds taking over.

The stories are untold.
Was there failure and bankruptcy?
Did the patriarch die of heart attack?
Did the matriarch with dementia move into a nursing home?

Was there a broken marriage and divorce?
Did the children move away?
Was there no one left to care for the home place?
Abandoned homes die a slow, wretched death

just like your soul will die
if you do not take care.
Pay attention.
Do not forget.

Marked

After the wrestling,
Jacob ended up
with a bad limp.

When Odysseus finally got home,
he was recognized by a long scar
on his inner thigh.

After the heart attack,
your heart needed stents
in two arteries.

We are all so deeply wounded
both inside and out,
and, if the gods grant us

any healing at all, it will be
hard earned.

We are all marked.

The Antidote to Pain

For Shannon Davenport

The antidote to pain is not anesthesia.
The antidote to pain is poetry.

And poetry takes time and space
and silence and dreams.

But before there can be poetry
there has to be stories:
stories of hunger
of craziness
of shame
of a father long dead
of healing the sick
of casting out demons
of taking a stand
of finding a long-forgotten path.

But before there can be stories
there has to be mercy,
sweet

        life-giving

mercy.

Inner Neighbors

1
Rilke's charge is true: "You must change your life."
We know it's true because
we all live with our brokenness, flaws, and errors
each day of our lives.
We all need help.

2
Harry Chapin in the *Cotton Patch Gospel*
has John the Baptizer roar:
"You got to reshape your life
for God's new order of the spirit is confronting you."
Yes, we must reshape our lives
to make them better and more whole
rather than remaining hollow, petty, and small.

3
William Stafford simply says: "You must revise your life."

4
And so it goes . . .
But here's the conundrum:
    There are parts of me that are burdensome
and ruined beyond repair.
There are parts of me that must change,
that must be reshaped, and that must be revised.

5
Yet . . . if I change my life,

then I am not me.
My wounds, my darkness, and my shame
are part of who I am — but not all.
Maybe what I must change, reshape, and revise
is the burden that
unless I change my life, I am doomed.

6
All that is required is to accept —
haltingly and graciously —
there are parts of me
that are unacceptable, unlovable, and imperfect.
Maybe I cannot change all those parts
but maybe, I can befriend them.

7
Maybe I can be kind to myself and live
with mercy, not terror;
with grace, not judgment and;
with compassion, not damnation.

8
Somewhere Jesus said,
You shall love the Lord your God
with all your heart,
and with all your soul,
and with all your mind.
This is the first and great commandment.
And the second is like unto it,
You shall love your neighbor as yourself.
On these two commandments hang all the law and the prophets.

9
Maybe I am supposed to do more than befriend
the ugly parts of me, these inner neighbors, I despise
    and hold in contempt.
Maybe I am supposed to love them all.

10
Maybe.

No Reason to Hold Back

The stents are working,
opening up the flow of blood
and holding back the night.

Now, open up your tear ducts.
Beware of those blockages too.
Let the cleansing salt work its way out

of your eyes and
let your heart be as open as it can.
There is no need to hold back;

there is no reason to hold back.

Change of Heart

The right coronary artery had two blockages.
Two stents were needed.

The ramus artery also had two blockages.
Two more stents were used.

Now the blood flows again.
Revascularization happens.

My heart changed.
So is my life —

        forever.

Both are True

The sun sets in the west;
light fades.
A half-moon begins to shine overhead
as dusk arrives.

Darkness will follow for a while and
then light will come again.
And then darkness. Again.
Both are true . . .

        even inside me.

The Tree of Life

In the dream, I am on a small hill
standing beside a massive tree.
The trunk is beyond thick;
it is ancient and holy.
Three giant limbs rise up, full of leaves and life,
forming a shallow basin in the trunk.

The great limbs reach skyward into the Heavens,
and unseen below,
the radical roots reach deep into the Underworld.
The sacred Tree of Life,
here at the center of the world,
is indestructible.

I begin to climb up the trunk.
I am being pulled toward the basin, to sit,
and to be held for a little while.
There, I know, I will be sheltered from the storm,
from the virus,
       from the fear.

There, I know,

       all shall be well.

The Unraveling

Your life changed when your heart attacked
without warning.
An anvil sat on your chest.
Breathing came hard and shallow.

The threads of your world unraveled.
The black dog watched
as you struggled through the fog
and the fear.

He stayed by your side.
Slowly Gratitude showed you how to begin
again, to re-weave your life
with threads of joy.

Angels Everywhere

It starts with fireflies in the yard,
soft blinking lights everywhere.
Then as dusk begins to settle,
the lights down in the valley glow.
The first stars shine in the heavens.
A deer appears at the edge of the woods.
Then off in the distance,
just behind the Sauratown Mountains,
she rises up through the clouds.

    There are angels everywhere.

And He Shall Reign Forever and Ever

I believe in walking the dog at night
when the spirits are alive and dancing.
I believe in music and in good books
that ease the hurting side of pain.
I believe in watching the moon rise
through Carolina pines.
I believe in sitting by a fire,
watching, doing nothing.

I believe in the realness of post-traumatic stress.
I believe in the quiet strength of the
        Blue Ridge Mountains.
I believe the worst thing is not the last thing.
I believe in the Psalms of lament.
I believe in rolling over, pulling up the covers
        and sleeping in on Saturday mornings.
I believe in the wild danger of poetry.

I don't pretend to know how —
or even what it means — but
I believe He shall reign
                forever and ever.

Gizmo

Abandoned on the Blue Ridge Parkway,
Gizmo bounded into our lives
with a ferocious protectiveness
and gentle spirit.

He watched over the family,
guarding and keeping.
His life-giving playfulness guided the girls
through the rapids of adolescence.

    He was a great dog.

Now Gizmo begins his final journey
down the Parkway.
I hope he finds all the broccoli, green beans,
and cheese slices to his heart's content.

He goes with our unbounded love
and gratefulness.

Prepare to Meet Thy God

The sign at the side of the road said:
Prepare to Meet Thy God.
It was a small sign, stuck in the ground, kind of crooked.
It's message usually means a personal apocalyptic judgment
where you stand before the throne of Almighty God
and are pronounced worthy of eternal life in Heaven or
else damned to eternal torment in the bowels of Hell.
It is supposed to scare the Hell out of you and
into accepting Jesus as Lord and Savior of your life.
Sadly, it doesn't work.

Actually, if you think about it,
you will meet your gods you really worship and believe in.
These gods are called by many names
such as Wealth, Youth, Health, Acquisitions, White Supremacy.
But if you look deeper, and trust your journey,
you will find other gods behind these false gods.
Hidden inside your soul are the gods
known as Forgiveness, Mercy, and Acceptance,
gods that give your life meaning,
that anchor your loves,

and make for eternal life here.

                Now. Forever.

Once There Was a Time

Once there was a Time
before time,
beyond time,
behind time.

Once there was a Time,
outside of time,
above time,
below time.

In this Time beyond time, there was Home
beyond home,
a sweet home,
before there was home —

Home where our souls waited to be born,
where we waited for the Three Sisters to spin
the twisted threads of our Fate
before our great adventure began.

In this Time before time
and in this Home beyond home,
we knew of love, forgiveness, and acceptance.
This knowledge would never leave us.

We were whole.
When our limits were finally spun and set in motion,
when we knew which stars were ours,
we began our lives

so one day we might return
when we were called Home,
called back into that healing balm of mercy,
whole once more.

Forever.

Insearch of Mickey Mantle

The young boy hustles to the corner drug store
when school lets out.
If he is lucky, Pop, his grandfather,
will be sitting at the counter with his buddies.
If he is even luckier, Pop
       will give him a dollar.

One dollar buys
100 Topps baseball cards,
with one card and one piece
of sweet bubble gum
in each individually wrapped
       unknown treasure.

Every young boy, like this one,
needs a hero —
a hero to admire, to inspire,
to teach him to be brave, to rise to the challenge,
to keep getting up, to have hope,
       and so believe the impossible is possible.

The young boy's hero is Mickey Mantle,
the great number 7
of the New York Yankees.
Mick is Zeus-like reigning
over the Mount Olympus of Baseball.
       His home runs were thunderbolts.

His arm a cannon forged by Hephaestus
and manned by Hercules.

Baserunners did not stand a chance.
His speed on the base paths
put Hermes to shame.
        Mickey stood taller than all the rest.

Late in the afternoon in the backyard,
it was always Game Seven of the World Series
with bases loaded,
two out in the bottom of the ninth,
and a 3-2 count.
        When the arch-enemy Dodger pitcher

would fire the last pitch,
the young boy would crush it
over the centerfield fence
just like Mickey would do.
The crowd would go wild.
        Mickey shone brighter than Apollo.

With the 100 cards the young boy runs home,
slams the door to his room,
and dives into the anticipation.
The bubble gum is crammed into his mouth,
piece after piece
        as he tears through the cards one by one.

He might find a Tom Tresh, a Clete Boyer,
maybe a Bobby Richardson
but no Mickey Mantle.
Never a Mickey Mantle card.
A hero is always elusive, just out of reach.
All he gets is a sugar rush and a sore jaw.

The young boy is now an elder
in the late innings of his life.
He no longer searches for Mickey Mantle.
There are no more Game Sevens,
no more dramatic home runs,
        just life — lived in gratitude.

For along his journey,
he learned he has his own thunderbolts,
his own cannon,
and his own speed.
He lived the work to which he was called.
        He shone as brightly as he could.

He listened to the pain of others.
He healed the sick,
cast out demons, and
sat vigil as people crossed over.
He cared for souls.
        He stood as tall as he was able.

The gifts were always there,
within, blessed by the gods,
waiting to be discovered.
His gifts were not like Mickey's.
They were different but they were his
        and that was enough.

It is always enough.

Wind, Stars . . . Moon

The wind whips and cuts
down the mountainside.
Even though it is spring,
the cold stuns.

In the heavens, the stars sing praises
without ceasing.
Then it happens.
Slowly she rises,

> hidden by a cloud,
> shining on my brokenness,

> > and my hope.

Cardiac Rehab

The nurses teach you about your target heart rate.
They check your blood pressure and ask how you are feeling.
They monitor your work on the treadmill and exercise bikes —
How hard are you working?
How's your breathing? Any shortness of breath?
Any chest pain?

But no one ever talks about the cold fear
sitting just below all the joking and false bravado
of the men.
Silence tries to keep the fear at bay —
maybe it's not real if we don't speak of it.
But the fear does not go away that easily.

It just goes underground
and shows up unannounced
in the dark hours of the mornings.

Shell-shocked

His countenance is full
of disbelief, grief, and fear.
He is having a hard time taking in
all the information the nurse is telling him
about the program and the exercise equipment.

Tears sit just out of reach, waiting their turn.
He nods and says he understands.
No, he doesn't have any questions.
He looks to be in his mid-50s or so,
younger than most of us in cardiac rehab.

I remember being shell-shocked,
numbed by the heart attack
and then overwhelmed by
the emotional aftershocks that crashed through.
Yes, the feelings come back

with all their wisdom and healing.
There is no shame,
no blame, in being shell-shocked,
We all travel down the road of life,
all the way to the Great End

                and Beyond.

Climate Change

An announcement from the Secretary of the Interior:
Warning...
You are in grave danger. Repeat: You are in grave danger.
This is not a drill.

Storms increase in intensity and
roll across the mid-sections of your soul,
bringing threat of high, damaging winds and hell.
Sea levels rise on both coasts.

Hurricanes form out in your wild oceans,
ready to slam ashore and
flood everything with their storm surge
of anger and venom.

The intense warming caused by contempt
brings drought to any feelings of kindness.
Like crops, these feelings wither and die
when not watered and tended.

Your interior life burns, noxious gases rise and
pollute the atmosphere.
Breathing is hard.
Your inner world is in great peril.

You need peace on earth.
    Peace in your earth.
        Peace in your heart.
            Peace in your soul.

Overlook

While the fireflies light up
the yard with their Morse code,
down below in the valley,
lights appear —

street lights, porch lights, and
lights in the parking lots.
They too offer their beacons.
Above, Venus shines in the heavens.

At dusk, overlooking the landscape
from the Blue Ridge Mountains,
you remain in awe of the beauty, the distance,
the hope, and the peacefulness.

You are where you belong,
among the fireflies,
the lights in the valley,
and Venus in the heavens.

Trust your destiny.

Under a Full Moon on Christmas Eve

The neighborhood is quiet this night.
There is no traffic and no sound.
Everyone is waiting and watching.
Everything is silent.

Like so many other Christmas Eves,
there is still no room available
in this broken-down, beat-up, shabby inn of my heart.
All the rooms are taken,

Occupied by my old friends
Shame, Fear, Pride, and Weariness.
I wonder if they will ever check out
and make time and space

for Mercy, Forgiveness, Laughter, and Acceptance.
Again this night the cold straw
and the smell of sweat and dung
await Joseph.

The moon watches in the darkness.
In the distance, I hear the Great Star.
Magi are coming.
King Herod stirs.

Come, thou long expected Jesus.
Jesu, joy of my deepest longings.

On the Way Home

You are crammed into an airplane seat.
Stuffed in with no leg room,
no elbow room, no psychic room.
     (Shame on the airline people)
Like your heart at times . . . no room anywhere.

But you listen to music.
Let Bach and the Beatles find their way in.

Words are in your heart.
Find them.

Feelings are in your heart.
Feel them.

Now and forever more.

Hawks fly over the Blue Ridge Mountains
at Fancy Gap.
Still, the words are with you.

Stories are waiting to be told and heard.

The trek towards home is always within.

The river is wide.
We will cross together.

November Afternoon

The late afternoon sun of November
shines through the oak trees
turning the yellow leaves even more yellow
and the red leaves even redder.

They are on fire
with the brilliance of God's gifts.
Lord, may my gratitude be likewise.

Waiting on the Moon

Under the gray winter sky, 18-wheelers grind
their way up the Blue Ridge.
Dusk drops through the cold and
the deer do not move,
waiting and keeping vigil.
We are all waiting
to see what gift she will bring tonight.
Through the clouds,
her light still shines. It is not hidden.
The clouds mask the fullness of the light,
just as our masks dampen our light.
But maybe the gift is that the light, our light,
somehow still gets through the darkness.
It still shines.
Our best selves are still here.

Young Children Know

Layered in toxic theologies of all ilk
spread across the centuries,
God remains hidden and unknown
from us.

Except for the young children.
They know.
They see.
They enter the Kingdom.

O Christmas Tree

You stand quietly in the corner,
carefully shaped in the mountains over the years
to point upward, upward to the heavens.
An angel sits on your top,
guiding our eyes to the stars.

The lights on your branches hold remnants
 of the dust from the long-ago Great Star.
They shine and lead us the way home.
There are the many totems of meaning,
placed carefully and gently on your branches.

They remind us of who we are and what we believe.
They are our histories and our stories.
So I watch you
and hear the whispered echoes
from the ancient past:

       Fear not.
             For unto us . . .
                   Peace on earth.
                       Goodwill.

Boys, Get Your Coats

"Boys, get your coats.
We are going for a ride. . . ."

It had been snowing for most of the day.
The ground was covered, the roads too.
Now late in the evening, school has finally been canceled.
My dad says the words
my brother and I have been waiting to hear.

We are going out.
My mother is not happy about this,
but she knows we will go anyway.
It's part of the dance, I guess.
We pile into Dad's Corvair.

He drives over to the shopping center.
The lights cast a quiet glow on the emptiness.
We take turns driving, hitting the brakes,
going into a skid, spinning, and sliding all over,
learning the movements of the car.

We laugh and yell, having a memory.
We have Dad to ourselves.
It is another magical night.
Now, sometimes late at night during the winter,
I would love to hear those words again,

"Boys, get your coats.
We are going for a ride. . . ."

Christmas Morning on Church Street

I was six years old, maybe seven, maybe five.
Near the Christmas tree in the living room
was the train set I wanted,
that I had asked for,
that I dreamed about.
The tracks were carefully laid out,
the engine and passenger cars were waiting,

even the red caboose,
ready to be placed on the track.
The magic potion that somehow made smoke
come out of the engine was added.
I was the engineer and the conductor.
All was ready.
The switch was turned on. . .
Nothing happened. Nothing. At all.

The plug was checked again and again,
the tracks were rechecked,
the engine reset on the track but still. . .
Nothing. At all.
My frustration went deep.
I howled and cried.
I raged.

I stomped on tracks
and kicked the engine.
It was a full-blown, five-alarm tantrum.
I was undone that Christmas morning.
Now many years later

I am ready to try again,
this time with another train set.
Maybe this one will work.

I hope — and pray — for a small Christmas miracle,
a miracle that will undo my long-ago undoing.
This Christmas.

Do Not Be Afraid

The almost-full moon sits high in the sky,
still watching, paying attention
while in the east,
Apollo begins his journey bringing
brilliant red, orange, and yellow colors
into the world again.

In the yard, four deer watch you
as you watch them.

They stand quietly.
"We see you,"
they whisper,
"standing there with a broken heart.
But be grateful.
We will not forget you."

Noli timere.

Lord, I Believe . . .

I believe in God the Father,
> maker of Heaven and Earth.

I believe in God the Mother,
> giver of life and home.

I believe in God the Grandfather,
> teacher of laughter and wisdom.

I believe in God the Grandmother,
> holder of tantrum and anger.

I believe in God the Brother,
> watcher of my back.

I believe in God the Sister,
> keeper of family lore.

I believe in God the Son,
> my oldest friend and fiercest foe.

I believe in God the Daughter,
> sustainer of courage and journey.

I believe in you,
> the great love of my life.

And I believe in me.

Lord, help Thou my unbelief.

One More Day

Sixty-two years. Three days
short of five months . . .
I have now lived one day
longer than my father.

I wish we could sit around the dinner table,
push back our chairs
when the meal ends,
tell some jokes, laugh, and . . .

Maybe we could have finished
the unfinished business between us —
or maybe not.
One more day does not really matter now.

What matters now is gratitude.

Christmas Lights

The Christmas tree is decorated.
The lights are up.
Hallmark movies play on the TV.
Presents are bought and hidden away until wrapped.
Christmas music of all sorts is on the speaker.

Just as the darkness will surely come this winter,
so will Santa.
Maybe so will Jesus.
Maybe Jesus will be born again
within the meager manger of my heart.

Heaven Was a Friend to Her

For Alice

Heaven was a friend to her
even as she knew of grief.
She was well-acquainted with sorrow and pain.
She had lived it all fully but still . . .

She drank from a deep well of gratitude.
Those who crossed her path,
entered her home,
and walked with her

on the journey
were met by an uncomplicated kindness,
a sweet laughter,
and joyful generosity.

She took care of Buddy and Boomer,
and Gizmo, Pepper and Silver,
and George.
and so many others.

Just as she fed the birds,
she took care and fed us.
She loved an off-color joke
and so she was the best neighbor ever.

And she was a friend to me.

    She was a friend to Heaven.

DNA Wins

You did everything you were supposed to do.
You followed doctor's orders.
    You changed your diet.
You exercised regularly.

You lost weight.
You took your medications.
    Still . . .
The stress test was not good.

The heart catherization
showed more blockage
    and less heart functioning.
Water runs downhill.

DNA wins.
Bodies wear out.
    But in the end . . .
All shall be well.

My Heart Is Not Failing

After the echo cardiogram,
the cardiologist said my ejection fraction
had only slightly improved, if that.
So I took another kick in the gut.

I was hoping for a different outcome
after all the cardiac rehab, exercise, diet, and new medication.
But now, the muscle is not pumping as well
as it once did.

The doctor used the words . . . heart failure.
After those words sunk in,
I knew my heart is not failing —
my heart is not cheating.

It is not broken.
It is not frozen.
My heart is just not working well these days.
The muscle is weaker

but the core of my heart remains intact.
The muscle is not my heart.
My heart is deeper, more true, than muscle because
I know of deep and abiding love.

I feel the salty tears of forgiveness.
I know of the tender mercies and memories of family,
I know the presence of my ancestors
as they still bless me.

Yes, my heart is weak
but that is only muscle.
My real heart is full of strong gratitude.
    That will carry me through.

Create in Me, O God

*Create in me a clean heart, O God,
and put a new spirit within me.*

The stress test showed evidence of more blockage
The cardiologist said another heart catherization was needed.

Lord, have mercy.

Wheeled into the cath lab and placed on a hard table — again —
the work begins as catheters are threaded into the heart.

Christ, have mercy.

Suddenly, they are finished:
no intervention this time.

Lord, have mercy.

The blockage is still there but
so is the good collateral circulation.

Christ, have mercy.

The collateral vessels have bypassed
the blockage, and so it will be.

*Behold, says the Lord God of Hosts,
creator of weal and woe,*

I make all things new.

No Job Title

You no longer have a job title.
You no longer have the big office.
You turned in your ID badge and keys.
You no longer have meetings on your calendar.

Your inbox is empty.
No one calls any more except
some clown selling burial insurance.
You said your goodbyes and walked out.

Who are you without the trappings of your job?
Who are you without your work?
It's easy, they say: just be who you have been
trying to be all these years —

a man who dabbles with words of poetry,
a man who believes
in the unknowable sacredness
of the soul,

 a man who knows the journey
is the way home.

What Are You Going to Do Now?

What are you going to do now, they ask?
What are your plans now that you've retired?
Are you going to travel? Work part-time?
What are you going to do?
But no one asks,

    Who are going to *be* now?

An answer is not required,
only asking the question.
That is enough.
I will figure it out
as I make the journey.

Misty Trail

On the third day of summer
the sky is a deep blue, holding only
a few remnants of high clouds.
The breeze makes the shadows
of the trees seem to dance.
Humidity is nowhere
to be seen or felt.
The cool temperature brings laughter.
You walk up old Misty Trail
with the one you love,
resting in the music of heaven.

    Nothing else is needed.

Rumi and Rilke

Rumi knew the cure
for pain was found hidden
within the pain.

Rilke knew the way back
to life after a wound
was only through the pain.

They were brothers
in the art of living
with soul.

Five Hawks and a Jet

While five hawks ride the great winds
along the Blue Ridge Mountains,
thousands of feet higher

a jet leaves a white vapor trail
across the sky.
Who's having the most fun?

My money's on the hawks.

Rainbow

The rainbow appears,
simply framed within the gray clouds,

its arc so close
you can reach out and touch it.

Maybe the Promise
is always like this —

this near.

This real.

Easter Moon

On this night long ago, I sat low in the sky,
full and red.
Something was up.
I wanted to see.
It was a night like no other.
It was cold.
The wind blew and
woke up the trees.
But no creature stirred.
              I think they knew.

Time stood still.
Then the earth shook slightly.
He walked out from the tomb into the darkness.
He stretched his arms and
rubbed his lower back.
He raised his head to look at me.
              I saw tears in his eyes
              and he smiled.

Then it started.
The angels danced.
The stars bowed.
Michael and Gabriel began to laugh.
They couldn't stop.
They laughed until they cried.
Nothing would ever be the same again.
Now there was Hope.
But then . . .
              people went crazy.

Callie Mae

One of my earliest memories is of
Callie Mae carrying me around on her hip.
We lived in the house on Church Street.
I had probably thrown a temper tantrum or two,

crying and pitching a fit.
My tantrums, I am told, were legendary.
Callie Mae did not mind.
She did her work around the house

somehow with me stuck to her.
I felt she loved me unconditionally, just like Granny.
She loved me for who I was and
for who I would become.

It was a tender acceptance
of my toddler tears and frustrations.
I don't know how long she worked for my mother.
I don't know why she left.

Others came. But it was never the same.
Now in this late season of my life,
I wish I could have told her
how much I loved her.

I wish I could have told her
how much she healed me

       by carrying me on her hip.

Take the Pain

Take the pain —
because if you don't,
you will lose them forever.

Take the pain —
even though you would rather
not feel that much.

Take the pain —
because it's your job;
you are called.

Take the pain —
because if you numb yourself,
you too will be lost.

Take the pain —
when it comes like a small wave
lapping at your foot.

Take the pain —
when it comes like a tsunami
crashing over you

and you don't know
if you will ever
breath again.

Take the pain —
no matter what because, one day,

without realizing it, you will

find yourself smiling,
smiling because there,
in the deep recesses

of your soul, are those
you have lost and grieved
so mightily.

There,
remembering you.
Loving you.
Forgiving you.

Blessing you.
Because you took the pain.

If I Were a Wise Man

I really did not want to make the trip.
It seemed foolish.
I would have rather stayed home and
studied my charts and made my calculations.

But they wanted to go.
They kept hounding me —
        badgering and begging.
They kept it up until I relented.

I just wanted them to shut up.
Yes, I would go with them,
following the great star in the heavens.
Let's just get it over with.

God, it was a long trek.
It was hot during the day and cold at night.
        I had no idea how long it would take and
what we would even find

when we got there,
wherever "there" was.
They said we had to follow the star.
I kept my mouth shut.

We stopped at the palace of the king.
Herod, I think, was his name.
        He was a shriveled, little man
with wild, rheumy eyes. Really paranoid.

I couldn't wait to get out of there.
I did not trust him — at all.
It was weird but
the star kept shining brighter and brighter.

It hung in the sky and
settled, it seemed,
        over a little podunk town called Bethlehem, I think.
Or maybe it was Nazareth. I forget.

It's been such a long time ago now.
I followed them through the narrow streets,
looking into the houses not knowing what they were looking for.
Finally, they stopped.

No words were spoken.
They took their gifts from the bags
        on the animals and went inside.
They did not even knock.

I stayed outside.
No way I was going in there.
I had a bad feeling now about this journey.
Something horrible was on the horizon.

I wanted to go home.
I don't know how long I waited.
        I heard a baby cry and
the father mumbled something.

They finally came back outside.
It was time to leave.
It took some doing but
I finally convinced them we needed

to travel another way home.
It felt too dangerous to go back the way we came.
      They did not say much about
what was in the house . . .

only that the baby was there and
his mother and father.
Strange it was.
A strange journey indeed.

We got home and
I could not shake the feeling that
      something majestic had happened.
But in my usual stubbornness, I missed it.

I did not know what it was,
only that it seemed something
was missing
deep inside of me.

Over the years as I thought about that journey,
I would somehow find tears in my eyes for no reason.
      I longed to make the trip again.
But it would never be.

So now as I search the heavens
in the dark of night
with my charts and my calculations,
I pray for forgiveness.

The child's name was Jesu,

      the Joy of our Desiring.

Leviathan

*Whale watching off Vancouver Island
(or reflecting on learning)*

Dive deep, my brother.
Dive deep and be fed.

This is the only way.
There is no other.

Three Voices

Inside of me —
      where exactly, I do not know —
live three voices.

The first voice roars:

      Produce. Do. Achieve.
      You need to attend this meeting.
      Policies and procedures need to be revised.
      There are deadlines to meet and
            reports that need to be completed.
      Budget variances should be corrected.
      Goals for the new fiscal year are due.
      Job descriptions should be re-written.
      Performance evaluations need to take place.
      All is of ultimate importance so
            don't forget anything.
      Your worth as a person depends on this.
      Don't make any mistakes.
      Produce more. Do more. Achieve more.

The middle voice sneers and mocks:

      You fraud.
      You know you will be found out —
            then what?
      You cannot do this work.
      You are a sham, an imposter.
      Shame on you;
            you always make mistakes.
      Who do you think you are?

The lowest voice whispers:

    You are forgiven.
    There is mercy.
        All shall be well.

Son of David, Son of Joseph

A Prayer

Thou art the pioneer and perfecter of my faith.
Thou art my Alpha and Omega.
Thou art the Resurrection and the Life.
Why, then, O Lord of my heart,
am I afraid of Thee?

Why art Thou far off and hidden from me
in my time of need?
Wilt Thou answer if I cry out?
Or wilt Thou turn and be silent?
I am afraid of both.

I beseech Thee, O Lord of my fathers,
to be gentle with me these days.
I seek something I am unable to name.
Find it in Thy mercy to show me.
Pour out Thy spirit upon me, Thy servant.

For I am broken, wandering, and bewildered.
Show me the path
which Thou wouldst have me travel.
Guide me, O Lord, with Thy mercy and
       forgiveness.

Thou hast given me joy undeserved
and likewise sorrow.
Help me to remember
that Thou art in both;
indeed that Thou art both.

Remember me, O Lord.
Be Thou the Christ to me as Thou need to be.
Be gracious unto me, sweet Jesus.
Be Thou my hope.
Be Thou my vision.

The Journey Home

The journey home will break you —
just ask Odysseus.

The journey home will also heal you —
just ask Parzival.

Or you could just ask me.